Mary Bowen   Liz Ho...

English World

Pupil's Book
1

MACMILLAN

Scope and sequence

Unit page	New words and speaking	Grammar	Grammar in conversation	Learning to learn (WB)
1 24	**Hello, Mr Jolly!** colours and toys	It's a car. It's red. Is it a doll? Is it pink? Yes. No.	Hello. Hi. What's your name? My name's …	Matching pictures; matching lower case letters
2 32	**Mr Jolly's Shop** school items	Is it red? Is it a car? Yes, it is. No, it isn't. It isn't a car. It's a van.	What is it?	Matching pictures; matching upper case letters
3 40	**Good morning!** transport	It is an umbrella. It is a red bike. It isn't a blue car.	Good morning How are you? I'm fine, thank you.	Finding the same picture; finding the same letter
48	Revision 1			
4 50	**Bella and Biffo** adjectives	He is sad. Is she Mum? Yes, she is. No, she isn't.	I'm happy. Am I Dan? No, you aren't. Yes, you are.	Finding the different picture; finding the different letter
5 58	**Mrs Goody and Pirate Jack** one–ten; food	regular plural nouns lollipops, cakes, sweets	How many are there? There are … There is …. Is there one …?	Finding the same picture; finding the same letter (direction)
6 66	**Happy Birthday!** nature	What are they? They're frogs. We're funny.	How old are you? I'm six. We're seven.	Matching pictures; matching words
74	Revision 2			
7 76	**Where is King Tub?** rooms in a house	prepositions: in, on, under	Where's my book? Where are my pens?	Identifying the missing items from pictures and words
8 84	**This is my family** family	I've got a brother. Have you got a sister? Yes, I have. No, I haven't.	Who is this? This is my brother.	Identifying the missing items from pictures and sentences
9 92	**Miss Silver** 11–20 eleven–twenty	He's got a plane. Has she got a car? Yes, she has. No, she hasn't.	I like grapes. How about you?	Sorting items into categories
100	Revision 3			
10 102	**The space rocket** action verbs	The rocket can fly. Can it jump? Yes, it can. No, it can't.	Stop! Look! Listen! Wait!	Sorting items into categories
11 110	**Up in space** weather	I'm flying. You're singing.	What's the weather like? It's cloudy. Is it cold?	Sequencing pictures; sequencing sentences
12 118	**Welcome home!** action verbs	He's eating. It's flying. We're reading. They're jumping.	loudly, quietly, quickly, slowly	Sequencing pictures; sequencing sentences
126	Revision 4			

Reading	Phonics	Listening	Writing skills (WB)	Class Composition
A toy shop descriptions of toys vocabulary: colours, toys	cvc words with short *a*	identifying objects	sentences: capital letter and full stop	naming and describing toys
At school descriptions of items vocabulary: school items	cvc words with short *e*	identifying objects	questions: capital letter, question mark	description with repeated question
Fast and slow information text vocabulary: transport	cvc words with short *i*	identifying; listening for gist/detail	colour adjective before noun	information text on transport
Jimbo; Ned, the snake poems vocabulary: adjectives	cvc words with short *o*	matching statements and pictures	capital letters for proper names	completing rhyming poems
Grandpa's shop a story vocabulary: food	cvc words with short *u*	action song	statements, questions	story with familiar setting
The garden descriptive text vocabulary: nature	words with *sh*	matching; listening for gist/detail	word order (adjective, noun)	descriptive text
A game a story vocabulary: furniture	words with *ch*	sequencing	pronouns	a story
My room descriptive text vocabulary: objects in room	words with *th* (voiced)	identifying; listening for detail	conjunction *and*	descriptive text
The space woman; I like … poems vocabulary: adjectives, food	words with *th* (unvoiced)	identifying from dialogues	adjective recognition	rhyming list poems
The Earth and the sky information text vocabulary: nature	words ending *ng*	following instructions	verb recognition	information text
What are you doing? descriptive text vocabulary: actions, weather	words ending *ll*	identifying characters	question words	descriptive text with questions
A birthday party a story with familiar setting vocabulary: actions, food	words ending *ck*	action song	word order (subject, verb, object)	a story with familiar setting

Welcome Unit
Hello!

1 🎧 **Listen and point.**

2 Now you!

3 🎧 **Listen and sing.**

4 Draw.

1 🎧 Listen, point and say.

a 🍎   b 🎒   c 🐱

d 🐶   e 🥚   f 🐟

2 🎧 Listen and point.

3 Write.

🍎 a a a a

🎒 b b b b

1 🎧 **Listen, point and say.**

g   h   i

j   k   l

2 Draw and say.

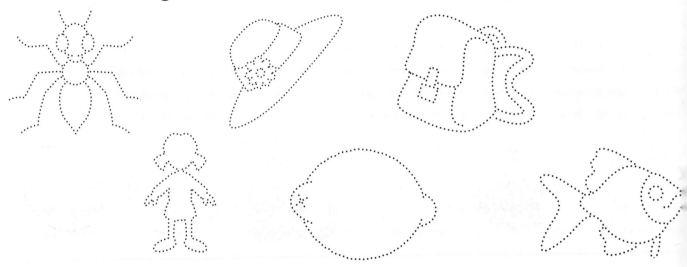

3 Write.

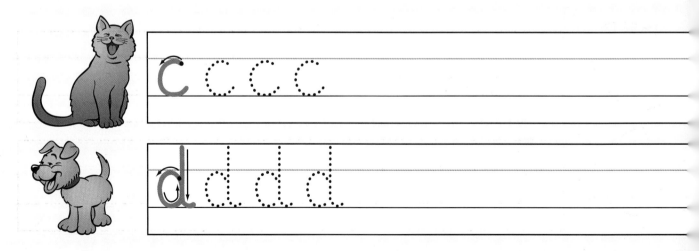

c c c c

d d d d

1 🎧 **Listen, point and say.**

m   n   o   o

p   q   r   s o

2 **Match and say.**

c   j   a   d   e   k

3 **Write.**

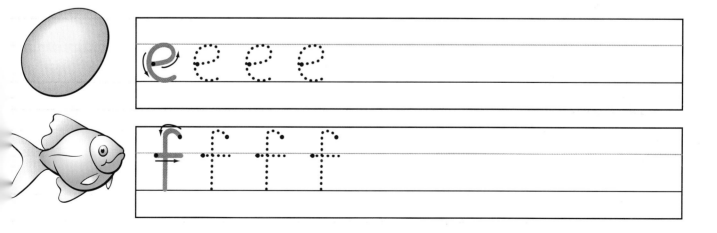

e e e e

f f f f

1 🎧 **Listen, point and say.**

t u v

w x y z

2 **Colour and say.**

3 **Write.**

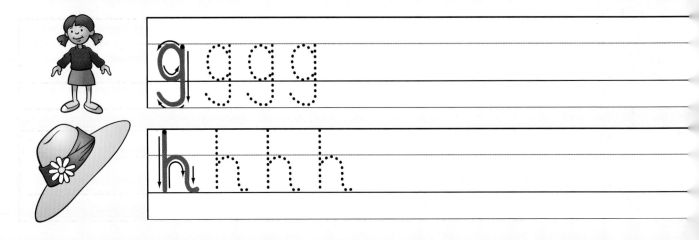

1 🎧 **Listen, point and say.**

a b c d e f g

h i j k l m

n o p q r s t

u v w x y z

2 🎧 **Listen and sing.**

3 **Write.**

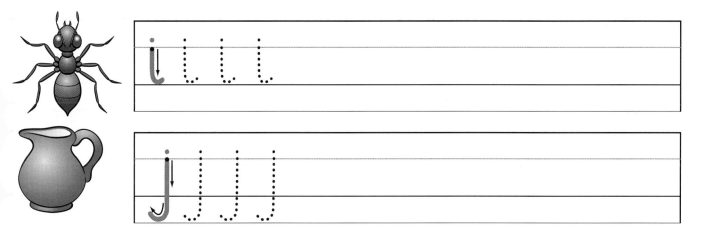

1 **Colour.**

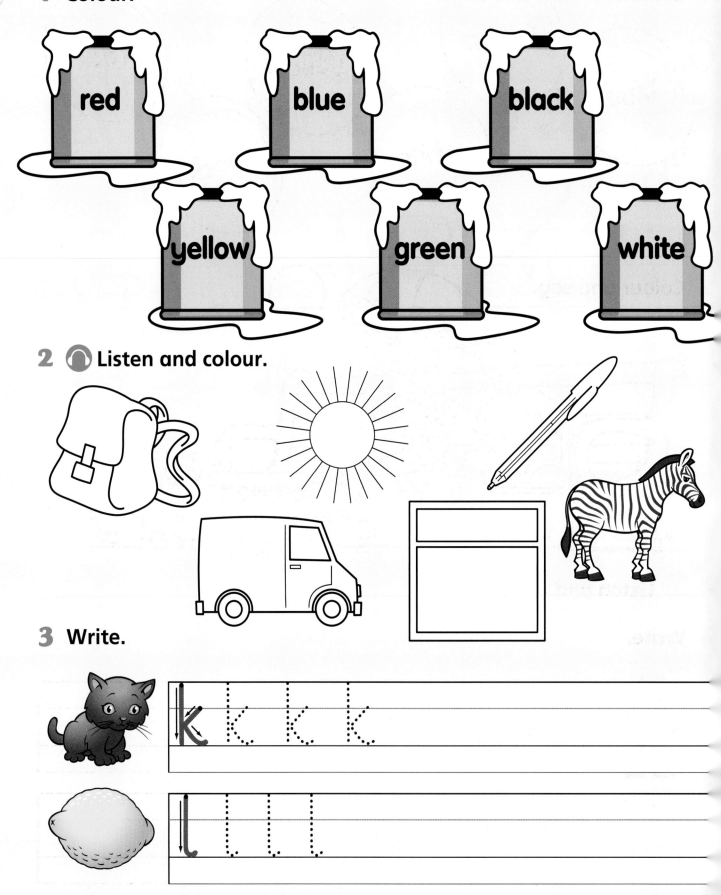

red

blue

black

yellow

green

white

2 🎧 **Listen and colour.**

3 **Write.**

k k k k

l l l l

1 Colour.

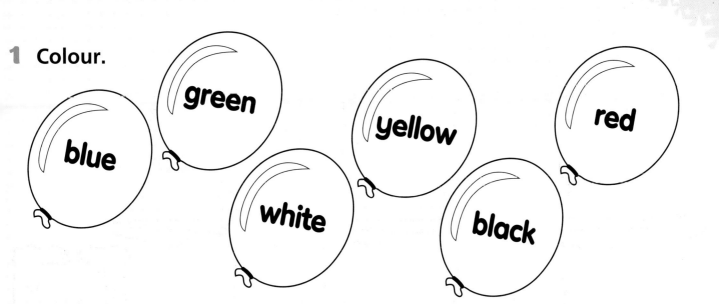

green

blue

yellow

red

white

black

2 Colour and say.

3 Listen and sing.

4 Write.

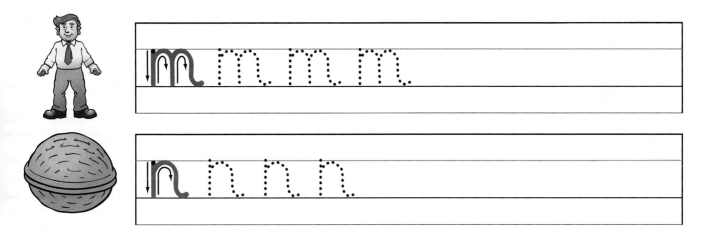

m m m m

n n n n

1 🎧 **Listen and point.**

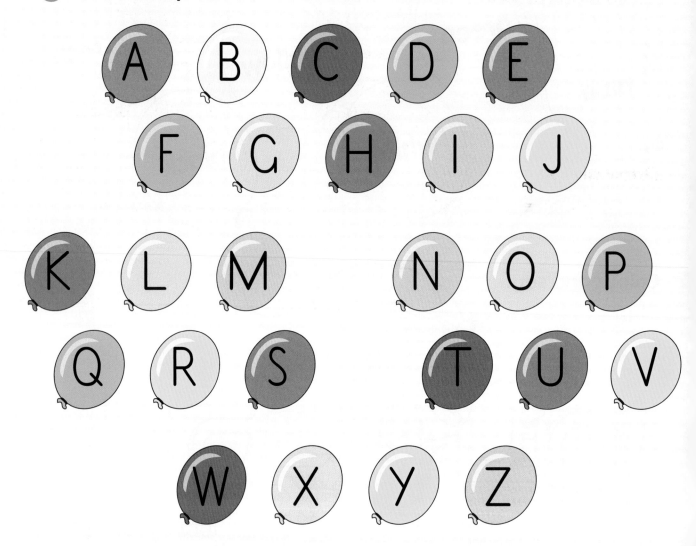

2 🎧 **Listen and say.**

3 **Write.**

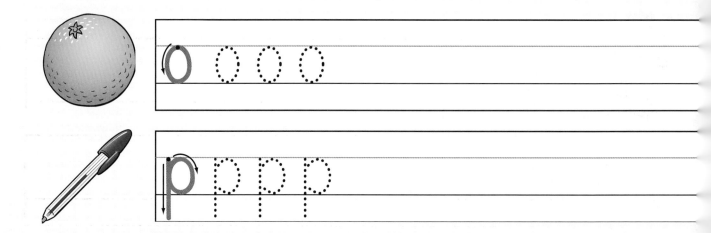

1  **Listen and point.**

2 **Draw and say.**

3 **Write.**

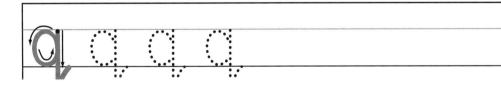

q q q q

r r r r

1 🎧 **Listen and say**

1	2	3	4	5

2 🎧 **Listen and colour.**

3 Point, count and say.

1

2

3

4

5

4 Write.

○ s s s s

 t t t t

1 **Count and match.**

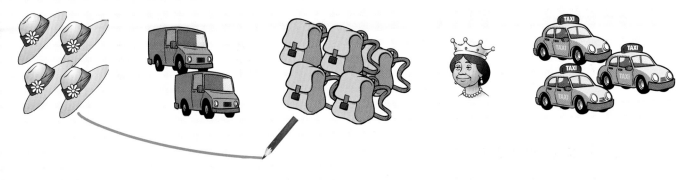

1   2   3   4   5

2 **Read, draw and count.**

4

2

1

3

5

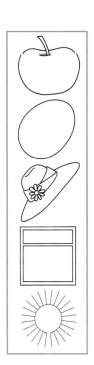

3 **Write.**

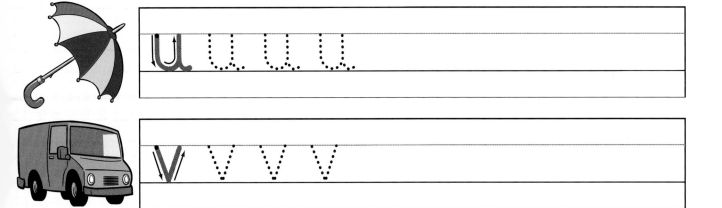

1 🎧 **Listen and say.**

| 6 | 7 | 8 | 9 | 10 |

2 🎧 **Listen and colour.**

3 **Point, count and say.**

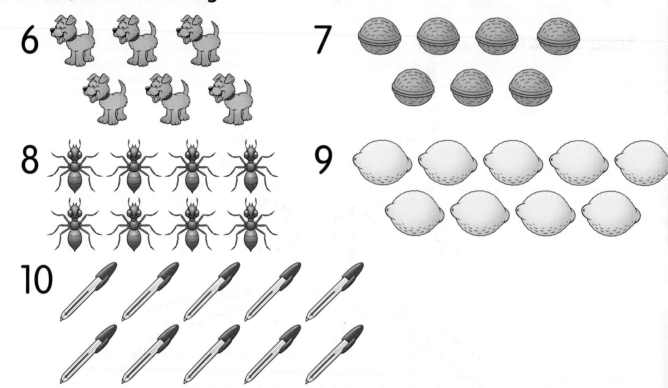

6

7

8

9

10

4 **Write.**

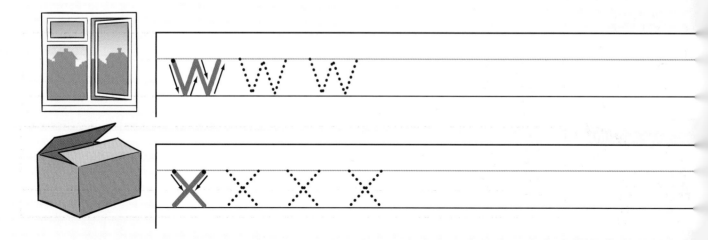

W   w   w

X   X   X

1 **Count and match.**

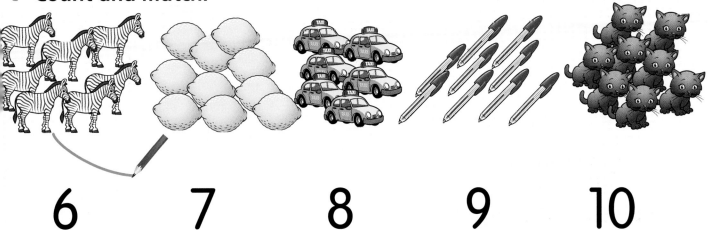

6   7   8   9   10

2 **Read and draw.**

3 **Write.**

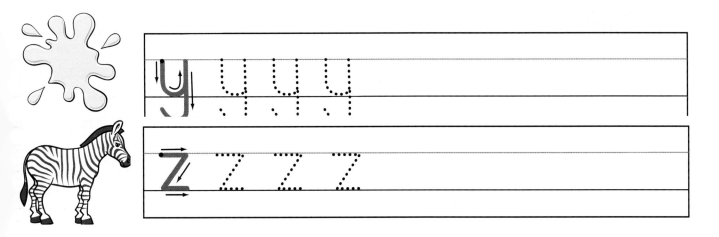

1 🎧 **Listen, point and say.**

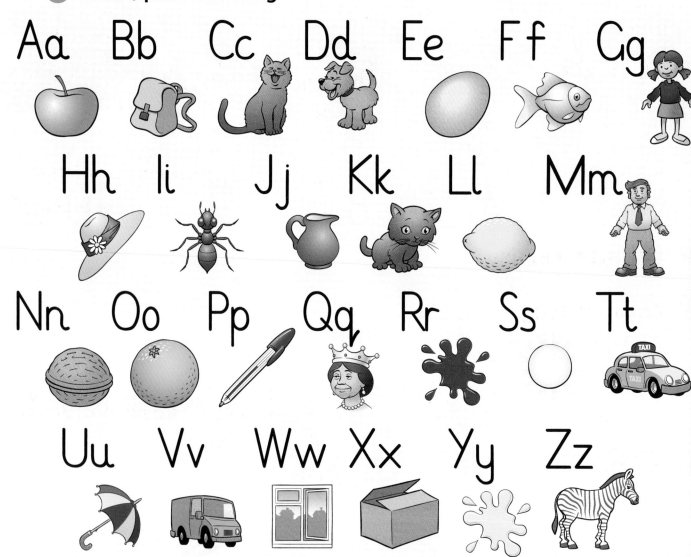

Aa Bb Cc Dd Ee Ff Gg

Hh Ii Jj Kk Ll Mm

Nn Oo Pp Qq Rr Ss Tt

Uu Vv Ww Xx Yy Zz

2 🎧 **Listen and sing.**

3 **Write.**

box   cat   pen

1 🎧 Listen and say.

2 🎧 Listen and sing.

3 Count and say.

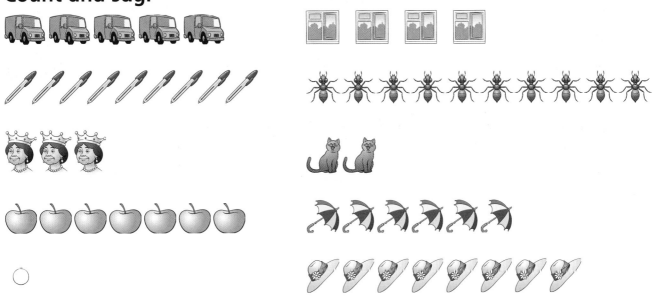

4 Write.

Meet the characters

Dad   Mum

Dan   Lily

Grandma   Grandpa

The Bodkin boys

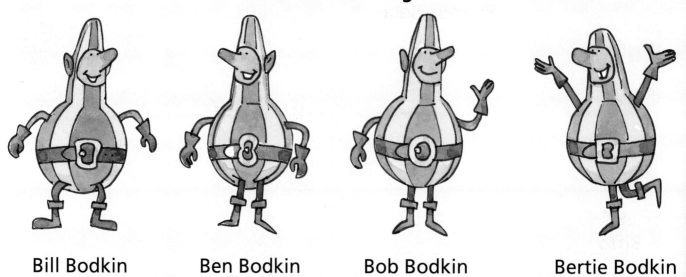

Bill Bodkin   Ben Bodkin   Bob Bodkin   Bertie Bodkin

Mr Jolly

Pirate Jack

Miss Silver

Princess Bella

Biffo

King Tub

Mrs Goody

21

Character game

1 Hello, Mr Jolly!

1 Listen and say.

- teddy
- boat
- car
- pink
- purple
- orange

2 🎧 Listen and read.

Look, Lily! It's a car.

It's purple.

Wow!

Look! Is it a boat?

Yes.

It's pink.

Look! Is it a dog?

No. It's a teddy.

It's orange.

Oh!

Hello!

Hello! What's your name?

Mr Jolly. What's your name?

Dan.

My name's Lily.

Hi, Lily!

Hi!

3 🎧 Listen and say.

Grammar

1 Look!

 It's a ball.

 It's blue.

Point and say.

1
2
3
4
5
6

2 Look!

 Is it a boat?

 No.

 Is it a car?

 Yes.

Ask and answer.

1
boat?

2
teddy?

3
dog?

4
ball?

5
doll?

6
cat?

Grammar in conversation

1  **Listen and read.**

Hello!

Hi!

What's your name?

Sally. What's your name?

My name's Alex.

2 **Listen and say.**

3 **Now you!**

4 **Listen and sing.**

Round we go
Round we go
Round we go
Round we go
Round we go
Hello! Hello!

A toy shop

It is a toy shop. Look, a boy and a girl.

Look. It is a ball.
It is blue and green.
It is big.

Oh! It is a train. It is red.
It is a car. It is small.
A boat! It is very big.

Look. It is a doll.
It is pink and purple.
A teddy! It is orange.

Look. It is a computer.
It is white.
Oh! It is a game. It is fun!

Reading comprehension

1 Read. Circle the picture.

1 It is a teddy.

2 It is pink and purple.

3 It is big.

4 It is a computer.

5 It is a game.

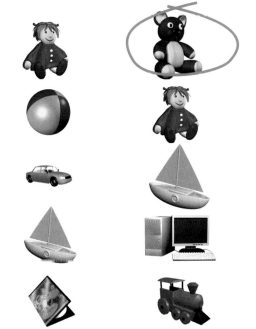

Phonics

Look and listen.

a   **hat**

1 Look and say.

h a t hat

c a t cat

m a t mat

2 Listen, read and say.

Dan is on a mat.
A cat is in a hat.

Listening

1 Listen and tick.

1

2

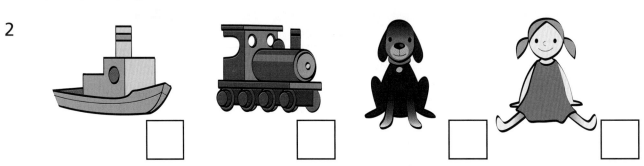

3

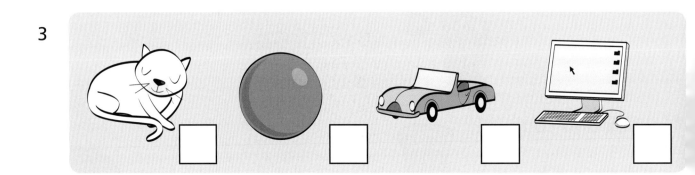

2 Listen and say 'yes' or 'no'.

Writing

Look.

It is a teddy.

a capital letter   a full stop

1 Look and write.

It is a _____ .   It is _____ .

It is a _____ .   _____ .

_____ .   _____ .

2 Mr Jolly's shop

1 Listen and say.

bag

book

pencil

kitten

rabbit

Mum

Dad

Unit 2 New words and speaking

2 🎧 **Listen and read.**

Hello, Mr Jolly!

Hello! Hello!

Dad, look! Is it a book?

Yes, it is.

It's big.

Mum, look! Is it a teddy?

No, it isn't. It's a bag.

What is it, Mr Jolly?

It's a pencil.

It's big.

Mum! Dad! Look at the hat!

Oh! What is it?

Is it a kitten?

No, it isn't a kitten. It's a rabbit!

3 🎧 **Listen and say.**

Grammar

1 Look!

Is it a teddy? No, it isn't. Is it a rabbit? Yes, it is.

Ask and answer.

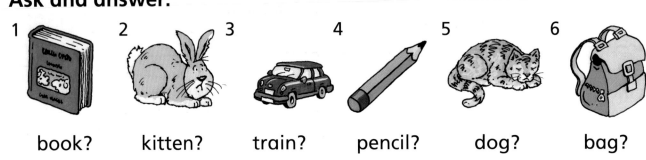

1 book? 2 kitten? 3 train? 4 pencil? 5 dog? 6 bag?

2 Look!

Is it a kitten? No. It isn't a kitten. It's a rabbit.

Ask and answer.

1 teddy? bag

2 car? van

3 book? box

4 cat? hat

5 pen? pencil

6 girl? doll

Grammar in conversation

1 🎧 **Listen and read.**

What is it?

Is it a car?

No, it isn't.

Is it a train?

Yes, it is. Look!

2 🎧 **Listen and say.**

3 **Play the game.**

4 🎧 **Listen and sing.**

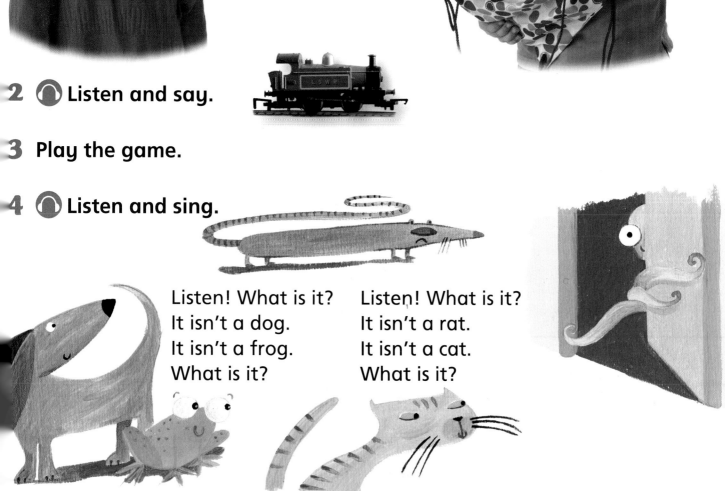

Listen! What is it?
It isn't a dog.
It isn't a frog.
What is it?

Listen! What is it?
It isn't a rat.
It isn't a cat.
What is it?

Reading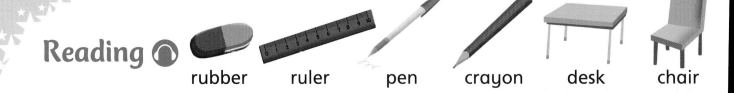

rubber   ruler   pen   crayon   desk   chair

Leo x one

At school

What is it?

It is a ruler. It is blue.

What is it?

It is a rubber. It is small.

What is it?

It is a pen. It is green.

What is it?

It is a crayon. It is red.

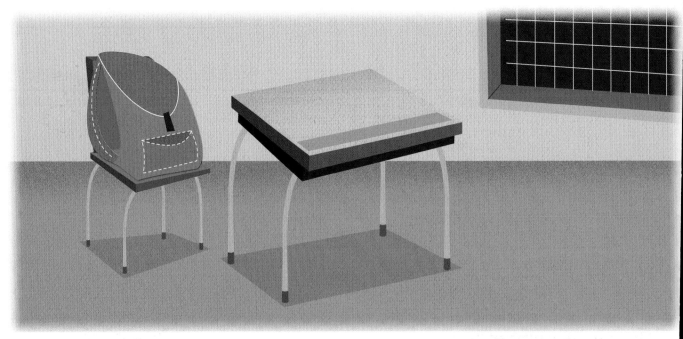

Look! The desk is yellow. The chair is blue. The bag is pink. It is very big.

Reading comprehension

1 **Read. Circle *yes* or *no*.**

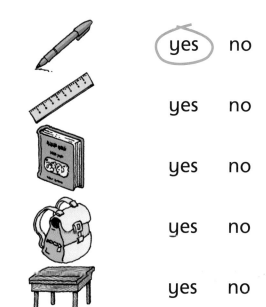

1 Is it a pen?   (yes) no

2 Is it a rubber?   yes no

3 Is it a pencil?   yes no

4 Is it a chair?   yes no

5 Is it a desk?   yes no

Phonics

Look and listen.

e   pen

1 Look and say.

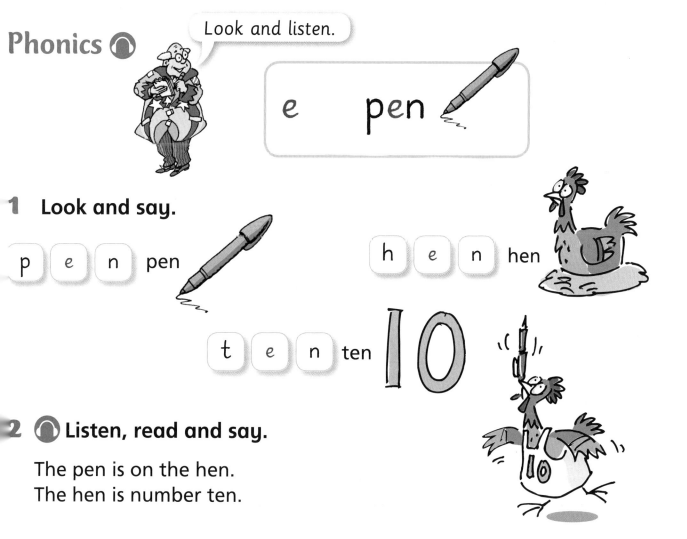

p e n pen

h e n hen

t e n ten

2 Listen, read and say.

The pen is on the hen.
The hen is number ten.

Listening

Listen.

1 🎧 Listen and write the numbers.

2 🎧 Listen and check.

3 Play the game.

What is it?

Brrm, brrm!

Is it a car?

No, it isn't.

Is it a van?

Yes, it i

Writing

Look.

What is it?

a capital letter   a question mark

1 Look and write.

What is it?

It is a crayon. It is red.

What

It is a _____ It is _____ .

_____

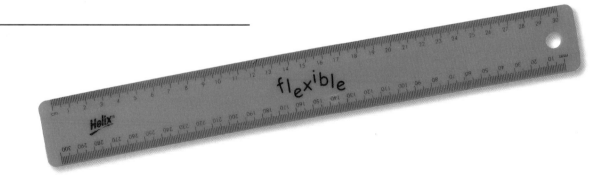

flexible

_____ .

3 Good morning!

1 Listen and say.

- taxi
- lorry
- bike
- umbrella
- Grandma
- Grandpa

Is it a lorry?

No, it isn't.

Is it a taxi?

No. It's a bike.

It's a yellow bike.

And look! An umbrella!

Hello, Grandma!
Hello, Grandpa!

Hello!

Good morning, Mr Jolly.

Good morning.

How are you?

I'm fine, thank you.

3 🎧 **Listen and say.**

Grammar

1 Look!

Point and say.

It's an insect.

1 2 3 4

2 Look!

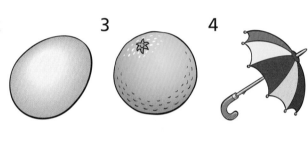

It's a lorry.   It's a red lorry.

Ask and answer.

What is it?   It's a blue car.

 1

 2

 3

 4

5

 6

Grammar in conversation

1 🎧 **Listen and read.**

Good morning, Mr Jolly.

Good morning.

How are you?

I'm fine, thank you. And you?

I'm very well, thank you.

2 🎧 **Listen and say.**

3 Now you!

4 🎧 **Listen and sing.**

Good afternoon.
Good afternoon.
How are you?

I'm very well.
I'm very well.
I'm very well, thank you.

Goodbye.

Goodbye.

Fast and slow

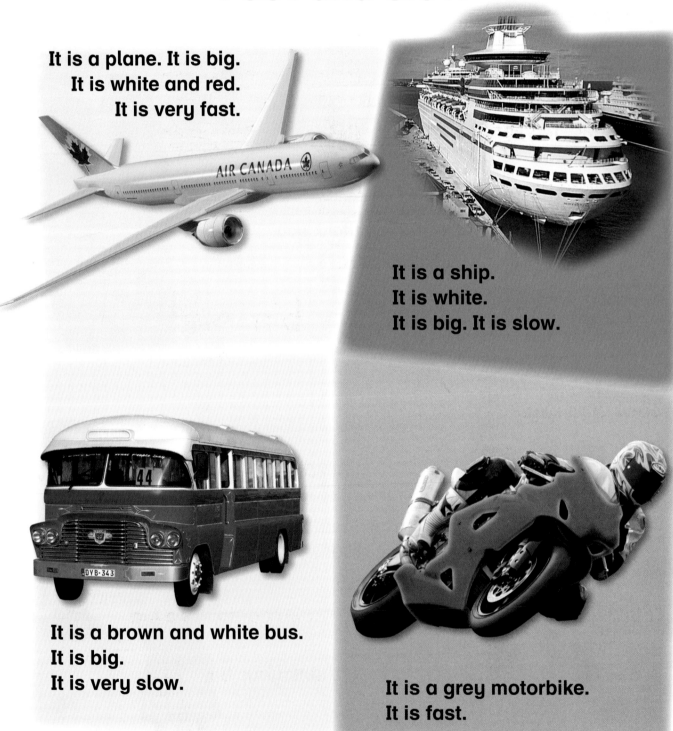

It is a plane. It is big.
It is white and red.
It is very fast.

It is a ship.
It is white.
It is big. It is slow.

It is a brown and white bus.
It is big.
It is very slow.

It is a grey motorbike.
It is fast.

Reading comprehension

1 Circle the picture.

A **B**

1 It is grey. It is fast.

2 It is big. It is brown.

3 It is big. It is slow.

4 It is big. It is very fast.

5 It is very slow.

Phonics

Look and listen.

i bin

1 Look and say.

b i n bin   t i n tin   p i n pin

2 Listen, read and say.

It isn't a bin, it's a pin.   It isn't a tin, it's a bin.

A pin in a tin.   A tin in a bin.

a pin   and a tin   and a bin!

Listening

 Listen.

1 Look.

A

B

C

D

2 🎧 Listen and write the letter.

1 _____   2 _____   3 _____   4 _____

3 🎧 Listen again. Listen for these words.

1 very well.   2 a white cat   3 a plane   4 fast

Unit 3 Listening: identifying scenes: listening for detail

Writing

Look.

It is a grey plane.

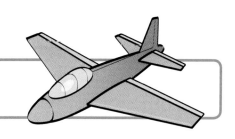

1 Read, look and write.

| train | lorry | car | | big | small | fast | slow |

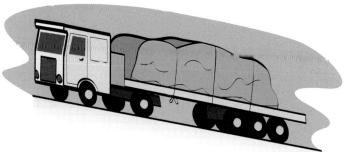

It is a blue lorry.
It is big. It is slow.

It is a _____
It is _____ It is _____

_____
_____ _____

Revision 1

1 **Say.**

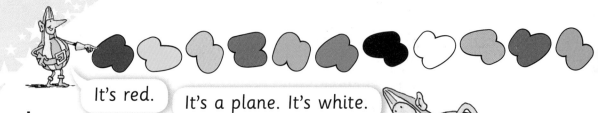

It's red.

It's a plane. It's white.

2 **Look and say.**

3 **What is it? Is it big? Is it small?**

4 **Read.**

The plane is white. It is fast. The ball is purple. It is not big. It is small.
The kitten is small. It is grey. The boat is red. It is not fast. It is slow.

Project 1 Toys

1 Draw ✏️ , cut ✂️ and stick 🖊️ .

2 Write.

3 Talk about the toys.

It's a car. It's fast.

It's a teddy. It's orange.

It is red.   It is fast.

It is big.   It is black and white.

It is a doll.   It is fun.

It is pink and white.   It is orange.

4 Bella and Biffo

1 Listen and say.

princess

clown

balloon

pretty

happy

sad

2 🎧 Listen and read.

Hello, Mr Jolly.

Hello, Lily. Hello, Dan.

Look! Princess Bella.

She is pretty.

Hello, Princess Bella. How are you?

I'm fine, thank you. I'm very happy.

Look! Biffo the clown.

BANG!

Oh no! Look at the balloon!

Biffo isn't happy.

Is he sad?

Yes, he is. He's very sad.

3 🎧 Listen and say.

Grammar

1 Look!

She's happy.

He's sad.

Point and say.

1  2  3  4  5  6

2 Look!

Is he Biffo?  Yes, he is.

Is he Mr Jolly?  No, he isn't.

Is she Mum?  Yes, she is.

Is she Grandma?  No, she isn't.

Ask and answer.

1 Mr Jolly? 2 Mum? 3 Lily?

4 Biffo? 5 Grandma? 6 Dad?

Grammar in conversation

1 🎧 **Listen and say.**

I'm happy.
I'm happy.

I'm sad.
I'm sad.

I'm fast.
I'm fast.

I'm slow.
I'm slow.

Happy. Sad. Fast. Slow.
Come on, everybody! Let's go!

2 🎧 **Listen and say.**

Am I Lily?

No, you aren't.

Am I Grandma?

No, you aren't.

Am I Bella?

Yes, you are.

Hello, everybody! I'm Bella.

🎧 **Listen and say.**

Play the game!

Grammar in conversation: *I'm … Am I …? Yes, you are. No, you aren't.* **Unit 4**

a clown

a short clown

a fat clown

an old clown

Jimbo

Jimbo is a happy clown.
He isn't very big.
The car is new.
The hat is old.
And look! A purple wig!

Jimbo is a funny clown.
He's very short and fat.
The bike is red.
The ball is green.
And look! An orange cat!

a snake

a long snake

a thin snake

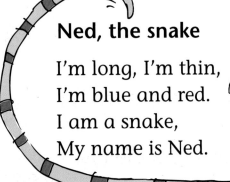

Ned, the snake

I'm long, I'm thin,
I'm blue and red.
I am a snake,
My name is Ned.

Reading comprehension

1 Read and circle.

1 Is he happy?	Yes, he is.	No, he isn't.
2 Is he thin?	Yes, he is.	No, he isn't.

3 Is it old?	Yes, it is.	No, it isn't.
4 Is it yellow?	Yes, it is.	No, it isn't.

5 Is it long?	Yes, it is.	No, it isn't.
6 Is it a rabbit?	Yes, it is.	No, it isn't.

Phonics

Look and listen.

o dog

Look and say.

d o g dog

f o g fog

l o g log

2 Listen, read and say.

Is it a dog?   Is it a log?   It's a dog in the fog.

It's a log in the fog.   It's a dog and a log in the fog.

Listening

Listen.

1 Look.

A

B

C

D

E
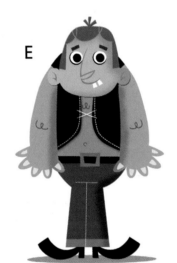

F

2 Listen and write the letters.

1 _____   2 _____   3 _____   4 _____   5 _____   6 _____

3 Now you!

He's a boy. He's funny.

Is it picture B?

Yes, it is.

Writing

My name is Ned.

1 Read.

I'm long and _thin_ .

I'm _yellow_ and blue.

I am a _fish_ .

My name is Lou

fat	thin	short

green	red	yellow

fish	cat	snake

I	L

2 🎧 Listen and say.

3 Read and write.

I'm orange and _____ .

I'm short. I'm _____ .

I am a _____ .

My name is __at.

white	yellow	grey

thin	fat	old

hat	bike	kitten

P	p

4 🎧 Listen and say.

Writing: completing and listening to rhyming poems **Unit 4** 57

1 Listen and say.

ice creams

lollipops

cakes

sweets

1	**2**	**3**	**4**	**5**	**6**	**7**	**8**	**9**	**10**
one	two	three	four	five	six	seven	eight	nine	ten

2 🎧 **Listen and read.**

Oh, look! Sweets!

And lollipops!

And cakes!

How many cakes are there?

One, two, three, four, five ...

Six, seven, eight, nine, ten.

There are ten cakes.

Yum!

Three big ice creams, please, Mrs Goody.

Oh ...

An ice cream, Jack?

No, thank you.

A cake?

No, thank you.

A lollipop?

No, thank you. Oh ...

3 🎧 **Listen and say.**

Grammar

1 Look!

One lollipop.   Two lollipops.   One cake.   Ten cakes.

Count and write the numbers.

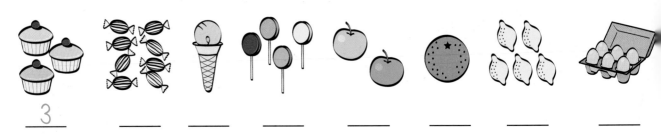

3 ____ ____ ____ ____ ____ ____ ____

Point and say.

2 Look!

How many sweets are there?

There are three sweets.

How many sweets are there?

There's one sweet.

Ask and answer.

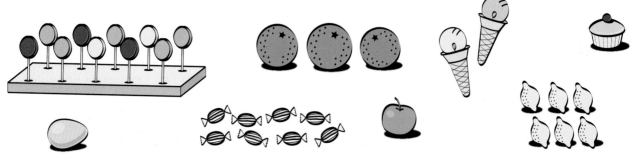

1 ice creams?   2 cakes?   3 oranges?   4 sweets?

5 eggs?   6 lemons?   7 apples?   8 lollipops?

Unit 5 Grammar: Plural nouns, *How many sweets are there? There are ten sweets.*

Grammar in conversation

next week.

1 🎧 **Listen.**

How many sweets are there?

Is there one sweet?

No.

Are there two sweets?

Yes.

One for you and one for me.

Yes. Here you are.

Thanks!

2 🎧 **Listen and say.**

3 **Now you!**

4 🎧 **Listen and say.**

Red and yellow, green and blue,
Orange, pink and purple, too.
Rainbow lollipops,
Lolli, lolli, lollipops.
Rainbow lollipops,
Just for you!

Reading

bananas   carrots peas   grapes   peppers beans   melons

● GRANDPA'S SHOP ●

Mmm! Apples!

How many are there, Danny?

There are ten.

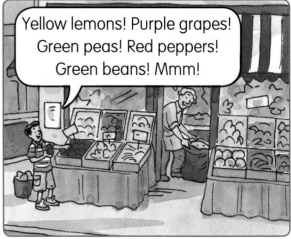

Yellow lemons! Purple grapes! Green peas! Red peppers! Green beans! Mmm!

What is it, Grandpa? It's big. It's round. It's green.

Erm … It's a melon.

Yes!

What is it, Grandpa? It's long. It's thin.

What colour is it?

It's yellow.

It's a banana.

What is it? It's long. It's thin. It's orange.

Is it a carrot?

Yes, it is.

… No, it isn't! It's a cat. It's Fizz.

Hello, Fizz. How are you today?

Miaow!

Reading comprehension

1 Write the word.

1

___peas___

carrots   peas

2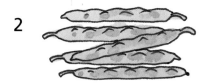

_____

beans   bananas

3

_____

peppers   carrots

4

_____

grapes   apples

5

_____

melons   peppers

6

_____

apples   bananas

Phonics 🎧

Look and listen.

u   j^ug

1 Look and say.

   jug   mug   bug

2 Listen, read and say.

a jug and a mug and a bug

a bug and a jug and a mug

a jug and a bug, a bug and a mug

a mug and a bug and a jug

Listening

Listen.

1 🎧 Look and listen.

Sandy   Andy   Pete   Paul

There are four boys on the wall
Sandy, Andy, Pete and Paul.
Goodbye, Sandy!
Bye, bye!
There are three boys on the wall.

There are three boys on the wall
👏 👏 Andy, Pete and Paul.
Goodbye, Andy!
Bye, bye!
There are two boys on the wall.

There are two boys on the wall
👏 👏 Pete and Paul.
Goodbye, Pete!
Bye, bye!
There's one boy on the wall.

There's one boy on the wall
👏 👏 👏 Paul.
Goodbye, Paul!
Bye, bye!
There are no boys on the wall.

There are no boys on the wall.
That's all!

2 🎧 Listen and do.

3 🎧 Listen, sing and do.

Writing

Look.

What is it?   It is a banana.

a question   a statement

Read and write.

What __is it?__
It is __round__.
It is red.

Is it a _____?

Yes, it is.

What _____?

It is _____.

It is _____.

Is it a _____?

Yes, it is.

_____?

_____

_____

_____

_____

6 Happy birthday!

1 Listen and say.

bird

flower

tree

fish

frog

present

card

Unit 6 New words and speaking

2 🎧 Listen and read.

Listen to the birds!

Look at the trees and the flowers!

They're very pretty.

SPLISH

SPLASH

Oh! What are they?

They're frogs.

Oh, yes! And look! A big fish!

Happy birthday, Dan and Lily!

Thank you.

How old are you?

We're seven.

Oh! A card!

And a present!

Thank you very much.

3 🎧 Listen and say.

Grammar

1 Look!

Ask and answer.

trees   flowers   kittens   birds   cards   presents

2 Look!

3 What are the words?

happy   sad   fat   thin   fast   slow

Grammar in conversation

1 🎧 **Listen and read.**

How old are you, Lisa?

I'm seven.

How old are you, Tom?

I'm seven, too.

Are you twins?

No, we aren't.

Are you friends?

Yes, we are. We're good friends.

2 🎧 **Listen and say.**

3 Now you!

4 🎧 **Listen and sing.**

Here come the clowns!
Here come the clowns!
They are big and they are small.
They are short and they are tall.
Happy and sad – we love them all!
Funny, funny clowns.

Reading

garden   sun   sky   cloud   pond   mouse   noisy

The garden

The sun is yellow.

The sky is blue.

The clouds are white.

The garden is big.

The trees are green.
The flowers are red and white.
They are pretty flowers.

Listen! The birds are noisy!
They are small.
They are blue and yellow.

The pond is not big.
There are four flowers.
They are pink and yellow.
There is one orange fish.

The small flowers are yellow and purple.
Shh! Look! Is it a rabbit? Is it a cat? What is it?
It's very quiet ... Oh, look! It's a brown mouse!

Reading comprehension

1 Read and write *yes* or *no*.

1 Are the clouds white?   _____

2 Are the trees red and white? _____

3 Are the birds quiet?   _____

4 Is the pond small?   _____

2 How many are there? Draw lines.

3   9   6   2   5   1   4   8   7

Phonics

Look and listen.

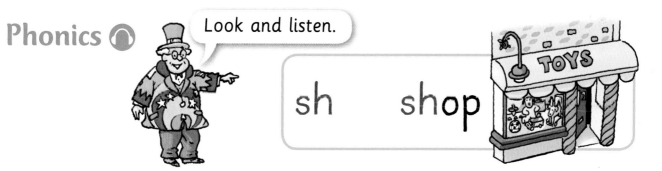

sh   shop

1 Look and say.

sh o p   sh i p   f i sh

shop   ship   fish

2   Listen, read and say.

A fish in a shop,
A ship in a shop,
Two shops on a ship.

Listening

Listen.

1 Look.

A

B

C

D

E

2 Listen and write the letters.

1 _____   2 _____   3 _____   4 _____   5 _____

3 Listen again. Listen for these words.

1 noisy   2 pretty   3 funny   4 quiet   5 happy

4 Talk about the pictures.

Writing

Look.

There are flowers four.

There are four flowers.

1 Talk about the picture. Finish the sentences.

The flowers are pretty. They are _____.

There are two _____. They are _____.

The _____ is _____ and black.

The _____ is orange. It is very _____.

| purple |
| red |
| cat |
| fish |
| frogs |
| quiet |
| noisy |

2 Talk about the picture. Write about the picture.

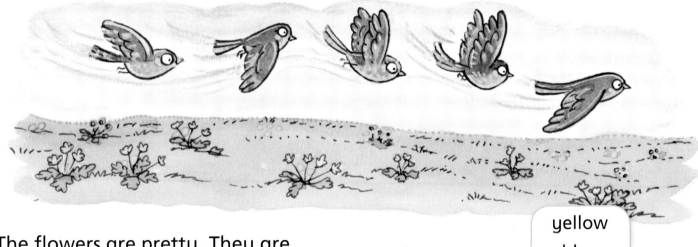

The flowers are pretty. They are _____.

_____.

_____.

_____.

| yellow |
| blue |
| five |
| birds |
| fast |

Revision 2

1 Look and say.

> How many are there?

> There are six lollipops.

2 Talk about the picture.

> The apples are round. They're red.

> The clown is funny. He isn't sad.

| round | quiet | pretty | thin | happy | sad | funny |

3 Read.

The garden is big. The flowers are pretty. The pond is small. There are three green frogs. There is one fish. There are seven birds. They are fast. Grandma is happy. Grandpa is happy. He is big. He is thin. How many boys are there? How many girls are there?

Project 2 A garden

1 Choose and draw.

2 Write.

3 Talk about the picture.

They're trees. They're big.

They're birds. They're brown and black.

7 Where is King Tub?

1 Listen and say.

castle

kitchen

living room

bedroom

bathroom

crown

table

stairs

2 🎧 Listen and read.

Dad! Dad! Where are you?

Princess Bella! What's the matter?

King Tub isn't in the garden.

His crown is on the table.

Look! Under the big tree.

Where is he?

Is he in the castle?

No, he isn't.

Is he in the bedroom?

No, he isn't.

Is he in the kitchen?

Is he in the bathroom?

Is he in the living room?

No! No! No! He isn't in the castle.

Where is King Tub?

3 🎧 Listen and say.

Grammar

1 Look!

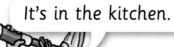
Where is the crown?

It's in the kitchen.

Ask and answer.

1 2 3 4 5

bedroom

bathroom

living room

kitchen

garden

2 Look!

The mouse is in the hat.

The bird is on the hat.

The kitten is under the hat.

Point and say.

1  2  3

4  5  6

Grammar in conversation

1 🎧 **Listen and read.**

Where's my book?

Guess!

Is it in the bag?

No, it isn't.

Is it under the desk?

Yes, it is.

Where are my pens?

Guess!

Are they in the bag?

No, they aren't.

Are they in the box?

Yes, they are. Here you are.

Thank you.

2 🎧 **Listen and say.**

3 **Now you!**

4 🎧 **Listen and point.**

Mike, Mike, on a bike
Fred, Fred, in a bed
Mabel, Mabel, under a table
Paul, Paul, on a wall
Lee, Lee, in a tree
Ella, Ella, under an umbrella.

5 🎧 **Listen and say.**

sofa

chair

cushion

TV

children

A game

Anna Jenny Joe Billy Fred

It's Anna's birthday. She is seven.
Where are the children?
It is a game. It is fun.

Where is Anna?
She is under the table.

Where is Billy?
He is under the chair.

Where are Joe and Fred?
Look! They are on the sofa.
Yes, they are!
Look again! They are under
the cushions.

Where is Jenny?
Is she under the TV? No, she is not.
Is she under the mat? No, she is not!
Where is she?
There she is! She is in the box.

Reading comprehension

1 Look again. Read and circle the word.

1 Anna is **in** (**under**) the table.

2 Billy is **on under** the chair.

3 Joe and Fred are **in on** the sofa.

4 Joe and Fred are **on under** the cushions.

5 Jenny is **in on** the box.

6 The teddy is **under on** the mat.

7 The doll is **under on** the TV.

Phonics

> Look and listen.

ch   chip

1 Look and say.

ch o p

chop

ch i p

chip

l u n ch

lunch

m u n ch

munch

2 Listen, read and say.

Chop, chop,
chips for lunch,
peas and carrots,
munch, munch.

Listening

Listen.

1 🎧 Listen and find the pictures.

Where are my glasses?

2 🎧 Listen and write the numbers 1–6.

3 Now you!

Writing

Look.

Where is Anna?
She is under the table.

1 Look and say.

2 Write.

Jenny   Where is Jenny?
She is in the plane.

Billy   _____ Billy? _____

Joe and Fred   _____

teddy   _____

pencils   _____

8 This is my family

1 Listen and say.

family

mother

father

brother

sister

space rocket

2 Listen and read.

Is this your family?

Yes, it is. This is my mother and this is my father.

Who's this?

Rosa. She's my sister.

She's pretty.

And this is my brother.

He's little!

King Tub! What's the matter?

I'm sad!

You're sad?

Yes. I've got a plane and a boat. I've got cars.

You've got six cars.

Yes, I have. But I haven't got … I haven't got …

What?

I haven't got a space rocket!

3 Listen and say.

Grammar

1 Look!

I've got a space rocket.

I've got a boat.

Find the words.

bird   plane   dog   doll

1

2

3

4

2 Look!

Have you got a rabbit?

No, I haven't.

Have you got a bird?

Yes, I have.

Ask and answer.

bike   dog   cat   computer   pencil

1   2   3   4   5

Grammar in conversation

1 🎧 **Listen and read.**

Look!
This is my family.

Yes. And this is
my mother.

Anna.
She's my sister.

No, I haven't.
How about you?

Is this your father?

Who's this?

Have you got
a brother?

I've got one brother
and two sisters.

2 🎧 **Listen and say.**

3 **Now you!**

4 🎧 **Listen and point.**

5 **Now you!**

grandmother   grandfather   lamp   shelf   photo   bed

My room

My name is Lily.
This is my room.
It is big.

I have got a bed. It is blue and green.

I have got a box. My toys are in the box. I have got three dolls and I have got one teddy.

I have got a lamp. It is green. It is on the blue table. I have got a computer and I have got five computer games. They are on the green desk. I have got a chair. It is blue. I have not got a TV.

There is one shelf in my room. There are two photos on the shelf.

This is my grandmother and this is my grandfather.

This is my family. I have got two brothers and I have got a little sister.

Reading comprehension

1 **Read the sentences. Tick ✔ the correct sentences. Cross ✘ the wrong sentences.**

1 I have got three dolls and I have got one teddy. ☐

2 My bed is blue and yellow. ☐

3 The lamp is on the green table. ☐

4 I have not got a computer. ☐

5 I have got five computer games. ☐

6 I have got a TV. ☐

7 I have got two brothers and a little sister. ☐

Phonics 🎧

Look and listen.

th   father

1 Look and say.

 father

 mother

 brother

2 🎧 Listen, read and say.

This is my father,
This is my mother,
This is me,
And this is my brother.

Listening

"Listen."

1 Look.

1 Lisa

2 Ben

3 Ann

A

B

C

2 🎧 Listen and draw lines.

3 🎧 Listen again. Listen for the words.

1 family   2 father   3 brothers   4 grandfather

5 sister   6 mum   7 grandma

4 🎧 Listen and sing.

I've got a dog. His name is Boo.
He's a good dog, too.
Boo says 'Bow wow', too.
I've got a cat. His name is Roo.
He's a good cat, too.
Roo says 'Meow Meow', Boo says 'Bow wow', too.
I've got a bird. His name is Woo.
He's a good bird, too.
Woo says 'Tweet, tweet', Roo says 'Meow, Meow',
    Boo says 'Bow wow', too.

Writing

Look.

I have got three dolls. I have got one teddy.

I have got three dolls and I have got one teddy.

1 Look and say.

2 Write.

This is my room. It is small.

_____

_____

_____

_____

_____

9 Miss Silver

1 Listen and say.

11 eleven
12 twelve
13 thirteen
14 fourteen
15 fifteen
16 sixteen
17 seventeen
18 eighteen
19 nineteen
20 twenty

space woman

2 🎧 **Listen and read.**

Come on! Up the stairs!

One, two, three, four, five …

There she is!

Who?

Miss Silver!

Six, seven, eight, nine, ten …

Who is Miss Silver?

She's a space woman.

A space woman?

Yes! And she's got a space rocket.

Eleven, twelve, thirteen, fourteen …

Fifteen, sixteen, seventeen, eighteen …

Nineteen …

Twenty!

Phew!

This is Miss Silver.

Hello!

Hello!

And this is the space rocket.

Wow! I like it!

3 🎧 **Listen and say.**

Grammar

1 Look!

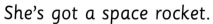

He's got a car.

She's got a space rocket.

Point and say.

1  2  3  4  5

2 Look!

Has she got a teddy?

Yes, she has.

Has he got a lorry?

No, he hasn't.

Ask and answer.

1  2  3  4  5

bike?   doll?   train?   clown?   plane?

Grammar in conversation

1 Point and say.

2 🎧 Listen and read.

I like sweets. How about you?

I like apples. How about you?

I like bananas. How about you?

I like cakes. How about you?

I like grapes. How about you?

I like ice creams. How about you?

We like sweets, apples, bananas, cakes, grapes and ice creams, too. How about you?

3 🎧 Listen and say.

4 Now you!

Reading

hair   eyes   glasses   tall   silver   space suit

The space woman

This is the space woman.
This is Claire.
She has got glasses.
She has got long hair.

Claire has got blue eyes.
She is tall, she is not fat.
She has got a silver space suit
and Fin, the space cat.

Eleven happy girls
and seven noisy boys,
twelve big bags
and twenty funny toys.

Come on, children,
Come on, up the stairs!
It's a silver space rocket.
Come on, up the stairs!

I like...

I like pears.
I like melons.
I like oranges.
I like lemons.

I like peppers.
I like peas.
Beans and carrots?
Oh, yes, please!

pear   orange

Reading comprehension

1 Circle the correct word.

1 Claire is the **space** / **silver** woman.

2 Claire has got **space** / **long** hair.

3 She is not **tall** / **fat**.

4 Fin is the space **suit** / **cat**.

5 The girls are **happy** / **funny**.

6 There are twenty **boys** / **toys**.

2 Write the words.

1 _____   2 ____ _____   3  _____

Phonics

Look and listen.

th   thin

1 Look and say.

th i n thin

th i ck thick

b a th bath

p a th path

2 Listen, read and say.

Thin bananas, thick bananas , one, two, three.

Thin bananas on the bath, thick bananas on the path

Thin bananas, thick bananas, one, two, three.

Listening

Listen.

1 Look.

A

B

C

D

E

F

G

H

I

2 Listen and write the letters.

1 _____   2 _____   3 _____

3 Listen and check.

4 Now you!

Writing

Look.

a happy girl
a yellow banana

1 Read the words. Choose and write.

noisy   purple   yellow   small   red   blue   quiet   big

In the garden

a _____ flower

a _____ pear

a _____ table

a _____ chair

a _____ bird

a _____ frog

a _____ mouse

a _____ dog

I like ...

I like _____

_____

_____

_____

boats

trains

cars

planes

2 🎧 Listen and say.

Revision 3

1 Read and say.

Dad Mum Jim Susie Grandma Grandpa

This is my family.

Where are they? What have they got?

Jim is in the bedroom. He has got a computer.

2 Where are they? Find and say.

3 Read.

Mum is in the kitchen. She has got a big cake. Susie is in the garden.
She has got an ice cream. Grandma has got an umbrella. It is pink. Dad
has got a red van. It is big.
The garden is pretty. There is a pond. There is one boat on the pond.
The cat is under the table.

Project 3 My family

1 Draw pictures of your family.

Find pictures of your family.

2 Write about your family. Choose words from the box.

tall	small	little	big	fat	thin		hair	eyes
short	pretty	long		noisy	funny		glasses	

3 Make a book.

This is my mother.
She has got blue eyes.
She is tall. She is not fat.

I have got three sisters.
This is my sister Hetty.
She is three. She is pretty.

4 Show your book. Talk about your family.

This is my father.
He is tall. He has
got brown hair.

I have got two brothers.
This is my little brother,
Fred. He is funny.

This is my sister, Jo.
She is eleven. She has
got green eyes.

This is my grandmother.
She is small. She has
got glasses.

10 The space rocket

1 Listen and say.

look

come

go

jump

fly

sit

moon

space suit

Listen and read.

Look at the rocket!

It's fantastic.

Can it fly?

Yes, it can.

Can it fly to the moon?

Yes, it can.

Can I go with you?

Yes, you can.

Hooray!

Come here, King Tub!

Jump in! Sit down!

You can fly to the moon.

Are you happy now?

No, I'm not.

What's the matter?

I can't go to the moon.
I haven't got a space suit.

Oh, no!

3 **Listen and say.**

Action verbs Unit 10   103

Grammar

1 Look!

The rocket can fly.

Point and say.   draw   jump   fly   sing   read

1   2   3   4   5

2 Look!

Can it jump?

Yes, it can.

Can it fly?

No, it can't.

Ask and answer.

1   sing?

2   read?

3   jump?

4   draw?

5   fly?

6   write?

Grammar in conversation

1 🎧 **Listen and read.**

Can we cross the road?

No! Stop!

OK.

Then look!

OK.

Then listen!

OK. Can we go now?

No! Wait!

Oh! A car.

All right. Now we can go.

2 🎧 **Listen and say.**

3 **Now you!**

4 🎧 **Listen, say and do.**

Stand up! Sit down!
Stand up! Sit down!
Stand up! Turn around!
Clap your hands and sit down!

Earth

star

beautiful

hot

live

count

see

The Earth and the sky

This is the Earth.
We live on the Earth.

This is the sun.
It is round and it is very hot.
You can see the sun in the sky.
It is yellow. Sometimes it is orange.

This is the moon.
It is round and white.
At night you can see it in the sky.

Look! This is the sky at night. The sky is black. The stars are white.

At night, look up! Listen! It is very quiet.
Can you see the stars? They are beautiful.
Can you count the stars?
How many are there?

Reading comprehension

1 Write the words.

1 _____  2 _____ 3 _____ 4 _____

2 Choose the correct words. Finish the sentences.

1 We live on the _____ .

2 The sun is very _____ .

3 The Moon is round and _____ .

4 You can see the stars in the _____ .

white	sky
Earth	hot

Phonics

Look and listen.

ng   king

1 Look and say.

k i ng
king

s i ng
sing

r i ng
ring

w i ng
wing

2 Listen, read and say.

A ring, a ring, a ring for the king,
Sing, sing, sing to the king.
A ring, a ring, a ring on a wing,
Sing, sing, sing to the king.

Listen.

1 🎧 **Look, listen and write the letters.**

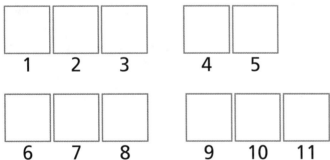

| 1 | 2 | 3 | | 4 | 5 |

| 6 | 7 | 8 | | 9 | 10 | 11 |

2 🎧 **Listen and sing.**

A bird can fly, a fish can swim,
A frog can jump, a mouse can run,
A cat can mew, a dog can bark
But I like to sit in the sun.
Oh yes!
I like to sit in the sun.

Writing

Look.

At night, look up!
Listen!

1 **Read the words. Talk about the pictures. Choose and write.**

Look!   Listen!

space rocket   moon   stars   sky

can fly   can see   count

noisy   fast   beautiful   black   white

Look! _____

Listen! _____

_____

_____

_____ ! _____

_____ ! _____

_____

_____

11 Up in space

1 Listen and say.

hot

cold

sunny

cloudy

windy

raining

snowing

2 🎧 **Listen and read.**

Wow! This is great!

What are you doing?

I'm looking at the Earth.
It's beautiful.

What's the weather like?

Down there it's hot and sunny.

And now?

Down there it's cloudy.
It's raining.

What can you see now?

Oh! Down there it's windy.

And now?

Oh! Look!
Down there it's very cold.

It's snowing.

You're flying very fast,
Miss Silver.

Yes. We're going to the moon.

Wowee!

3 🎧 **Listen and say.**

Grammar

1 Look!

I'm flying.

Find the words. looking jumping singing standing listening

1 I'm

2 I'm

3 I'm

4 I'm

5 I'm

2 Look!

You're singing.

No!

You're standing.

Yes!

Now you.

singing standing flying jumping
pointing reading listening drawing

Grammar in conversation

1 🎧 **Listen and read.**

Hello?

Hello, James. It's Grandma here.

Hello, Grandma.

What are you doing?

I'm reading a book.

What's the weather like there?

It's cloudy.

Is it cold?

No, it isn't.

Is Mum there?

Yes, she is. Mum!

Goodbye, James.

Bye, Grandma.

2 🎧 **Listen and say.**

3 **Now you!**

4 🎧 **Listen and sing.**

The rain is falling, the clouds are grey.
It's a cold, wet, windy day.
But look up in the sky. What can you see?
The sun! The sun!
And a rainbow, a rainbow, a rainbow for you and me!

Reading

kite snowman sunglasses hold eat play

What are you doing?

What are you doing, Amy?

I am holding an umbrella.
It is raining.
What colour is my umbrella?

What are you doing, Jill?

I am going to school.
It is cold! I have got a hat.
What colour is it?

What are you doing, Betty?

I am looking at the boats.
It is sunny. I have got sunglasses.
How many boats are there?

What are you doing, Tom?

I am holding my kite.
It is windy!
How many kites are there?

What are you doing, Harry?

I am playing in the garden.
It is snowing. Look at my snowman!
Where is the bird?

What are you doing, Max?

I am eating an ice cream.
It is very hot today.
Mmm! I like ice cream!
It is cold!

Reading comprehension

1 Read the sentences. Answer the questions.

1 I am holding my kite. Who am I?   _Tom_

2 It is not snowing. I have got a hat. Who am I?   _____

3 It is cold. I am playing in the garden. Who am I?   _____

4 It is sunny. I am eating an ice cream. Who am I?   _____

5 It is not sunny. I am holding an umbrella. Who am I?   _____

6 I am sitting in a boat. Who am I?   _____

Phonics

Look and listen.

ll   bell

1 Look and say.

b e ll bell    w e ll well

h i ll hill   d o ll doll

2 Listen, read and say.

Up the hill
to the well.
Find a doll.
Ring the bell.

Listening

Listen.

1 🎧 **Look, listen and point.**

| Ann | Meg | Sue | Amy | Ned | Jim | Sam | Ben |

2 🎧 **Listen and write the names.**

3 **Play the game.**

Who am I?

You're drawing a picture. No.

You're singing a song. Yes.

You're Sue. Yes.

Writing

Look.

Where is the fish?
What colour is the fish?
How many flowers are there?

1 Read the words.

playing	holding
room	plane
raining	windy

Write.

What are you doing, Sam?

I am playing in my room.

_____

_____?

2 Read the words.

| standing | eating |
| sunny | hot |

Write. | boat | ice cream |

_____, Betty?

_____

_____

_____?

12 Welcome home!

1 Listen and say.

jumping

laughing

singing

loudly

party

2 🎧 Listen and read.

Look! King Tub and Miss Silver!

They're laughing.

Welcome home!

Welcome home!

Look at King Tub!

He's very happy.

He's jumping up and down.

Miss Silver is happy, too.

Yes. She's singing loudly.

Thank you, Miss Silver.

Not at all.

I like your space rocket very much.

Are you happy now?

Yes, I am. I'm very happy.

Hooray! Hooray!

Come on, everyone! It's time for a party!

Hooray! Hooray! Welcome home!

3 🎧 Listen and say.

Grammar

1 Look!

He's reading.

She's drawing.

It's flying.

Match and write the letters.

1 He's laughing. ____

2 It's jumping. ____

3 She's reading. ____

A

B

C

2 Look! We're eating apples.

They're eating bananas.

Find the words and say.

singing   reading   drawing   jumping   standing   eating

1

2

We're …   We're …   We're …   They're …   They're …   They're …

Grammar in conversation

1 **Read and match.**

1 He's singing loudly.

2 She's talking quietly.

3 It's flying quickly.

4 They're walking slowly.

A

B

C

D

2 **Listen and read.**

| loudly | quietly | quickly | slowly |

Let's play a game. Choose a word.

OK.

Can you talk like this?

Good morning.

Can you count like this?

1 ... 2 ... 3 ... 4 ...

You're counting slowly.
The word is *slowly*.

That's right.

3 **Listen and say.**

4 **Now you!**

orange juice

open

drink

walk

A birthday party for Pete

> This is a present for Pete.

> This is a card for Pete.

Billy and Milly are going to a birthday party. Billy is holding a present. Milly is holding a card.

> Please, come in!

> Happy birthday, Pete!

Pete is opening the door quickly. He is laughing loudly. He is very happy.

> What is it?

> Is it a boat?

> It's a plane! Thank you!

The children are looking at Pete's birthday present. Pete is opening the present.

> Look at the plane!

The red plane is flying. The children are laughing and pointing.

> This is fun!

> Come on!

Now the children are playing in the garden. They are walking slowly on the log. They are jumping.

> I like cakes!

> I like orange juice!

The children have got funny hats. They are eating and they are drinking. It is a fantastic party!

Reading comprehension

1 Answer the questions.

1 What is Milly holding? _____

2 What is Billy holding? _____

3 Who is opening the door? _____

4 What is the present for Pete? _____

5 Where are the children playing? _____

6 How many children are there? _____

7 What are the children drinking? _____

Phonics 🎧

> Look and listen.

ck   sack

1 Look and say.

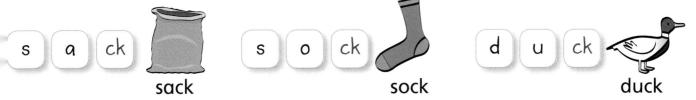

s a ck   s o ck   d u ck

sack   sock   duck

2 🎧 Listen, read and say.

The sock is on the duck.
The sack is in the sock.
The duck is in the sack.
Quack! Quack! Quack!

Listening

1  **Listen.**

We're on holiday.
We're having fun.

We're eating ice creams.
We're on holiday.
We're having fun.

We're playing football.
We're eating ice creams.
We're on holiday.
We're having fun.

We're running and jumping.
We're playing football.
We're eating ice creams.
We're on holiday.
We're having fun.

We are swimming.
We're running and jumping.
We're playing football.
We're eating ice creams.
We're on holiday.
We're having fun.

We are laughing.
We are swimming.
We're running and jumping.
We're playing football.
We're eating ice creams.
We're on holiday.
We're having fun.

We're on holiday.
We're having FUN.

2 **Listen and sing.**

Writing

"Look.

Pete is opening the door."

1 Read the words. Talk about the pictures. Write the story.

| playing   flying   looking |

_____

_____

| looking   jumping   quickly |

_____

_____

| cannot fly   looking   holding |

_____

_____

_____

| opening   laughing   loudly   new |

_____

_____

_____

Revision 4

1 **What is the weather like? What are the children doing?**

It's sunny. It's hot.

Pete is holding a plane.

2 **Find these things. Where are they?**

3 **Read.**

In picture 1 it is hot and sunny. The children are looking at the fish. In picture 2 it is windy and it is raining. Pete and Billy are standing under a tree. In picture 3 it is snowing and it is cold. There are twelve birds in the garden. In picture 4 the children are looking at the stars. It is night. They can see the big white moon.

Project 4 A weather picture

1 **What is the weather like? Choose.**

> windy   sunny   cloudy   raining   snowing   hot   cold

2 **Who is in the picture? Choose.**

> brother   sister   friend   mother   father   grandmother   grandfather

3 **What are they doing? Choose.**

> jumping   looking   pointing   standing
> reading   drawing   holding   playing   laughing

4 **Draw and write.**

5 **Talk about the picture.**

It is windy and it is cloudy. It is not cold. This is my friend, Anna, and this is me. We are jumping. This is my brother, Sam. He is flying a kite.

It is sunny and it is hot. This is my sister. She is standing.

This is my grandmother. She is reading.

This is my grandfather. He is singing.

This is my brother. This is my sister. They are jumping.

Macmillan Education
4 Crinan Street
London N1 9XW
A division of Macmillan Publishers Limited
Companies and representatives throughout the world

ISBN 978-023-002459-5

First published 2009

Concept design by Anthony Godber
Design by Ken Vail Graphic Design, Cambridge
Illustrated by Beehive Illustration (Neil Chapman, Robin Edmonds, Mark Ruffle,
Mark Turner); The Bright Agency (Barbara Vagnozzi); Graham Cameron Illustration
(Chris Petty); Andy Cooke; Rasha al Hakim; Sylvie Poggio Artists Agency
(Rita Giannetti, Lisa Smith); David Woodroffe.
Cover design by Oliver Design

The authors and publishers would like to thank the following for permission to reproduce
their photographic material:
Alamy/Stephen Roberts Photography p35; Alamy/ Ian Dagnall p44(bl); Alamy/
WoodyStock/Wolfgang Filzwieser p44(br); Alamy/Jeff Smith P106(mb); Alamy/Photo
Network/John Sanford pp106(b), 109.
Brand X P106(tm)
Courtesy of Air Canada p44(tl)
NASA/JSC p106(t)
Superstock p44(tr)

Cover Photography: Clark Wiseman/www.studio-8.co.uk

The publishers would like to thank the following for their participation in the development
of this course:
In Egypt – Inas Agiz, Salma Ahmed, Hekmat Aly, Suzi Balaban, Mohamed Eid, Bronwen
El Kholy, Mostafa El Makhzangy, Hala Fouad, Jonathan French, Nashaat Nageeb Gendy,
Hisham Howeedy, Saber Lamey, Heidi Omara, Maha Radwan, Amany Shawkey, Christine
Abu Sitta, Ali Abdel Wahab
In Russia – Tatiana Antonova, Elena Belonozhkina, Galina Dragunova, Irina Filonenko,
Marina Gaisina, Maria Goretaya, Oksana Guzhnovskaya, Irina Kalinina, Olga
Kligerman, Galina Kornikova, Lidia Kosterina, Sergey Kozlov, Irina Larionova, Irina
Lenchenko, Irina Lyubimova, Karine Makhmuryan, Maria Pankina, Anna Petrenkova,
Elena Plisko, Natalia Vashchenko, Angelika Vladyko

Commissioned photography by Paul Bricknell

Printed and bound in Italy by Rotolito Lombarda

2019 2018 2017
33